Handwriting
Secrets
Revealed

Handwriting Secrets Revealed

SEAN CALLERY

WARD LOCK

A WARD LOCK BOOK

This edition published in the UK 1994
by Ward Lock
Villiers House
41/47 Strand
LONDON
WC2N 5JE

A Cassell Imprint

Copyright © Text and illustrations Ward Lock 1994

This book was previously published in 1989

Distributed in the United States
by Sterling Publishing Co., Inc.
387 Park Avenue South, New York, NY 10016-8810

Distributed in Australia
by Capricorn Link (Australia) Pty Ltd
2/13 Carrington Road, Castle Hill NSW 2154

A British Library Cataloguing in Publication Data block for this
book may be obtained from the British Library

ISBN 0 7063 7328 6

Typeset by Columns of Reading Ltd
Printed and bound in Great Britain by Harper Collins

CONTENTS

INTRODUCTION

How much do you really know about yourself, your friends, your lover, your children? Everything we do says something about us, from the way we shake hands, to how we drive a car. But many of our actions are designed to conceal our true nature, to hide what we actually think and feel.

Finding out what someone is really like, their hopes and fears, their emotions and aspirations, is impossible if we only look at how they behave or what they say. We have to go deeper to find the truth about them.

Graphology (the study of character from handwriting) takes us into the underworld of the subconscious, to the secrets we keep even from ourselves. It works because handwriting is body language on the page. It reflects all the character traits of the writer, their dreams, foibles, intelligence – everything that makes them who they are – and it is virtually impossible for anyone to prevent their handwriting from revealing these secrets.

THE BENEFITS OF GRAPHOLOGY

The benefits of skill in graphology are numerous. It provides a better understanding of ourselves, those who are close to us, those we compete with, helps parents to monitor the progress of their children – it can even spot the onset of an illness before the symptoms have appeared!

Graphology is widely understood and used in many countries. In many parts of Europe and the USA graphologists are brought in by large firms to help assess job applicants. Half the major companies in Germany ask a graphologist for advice on potential employees, and the figure is even higher in Holland. Those firms know that an expert study of your letter of application reveals far more than the words on the page. They may end up knowing more about you than you do, without even meeting you!

Now you can join in and, by careful, objective analysis of a page of handwriting, find out more about the writer in a few hours than some of us ever know in a lifetime.

There is nothing sinister about the study of character from handwriting, and it is a great shame that graphology books seem to be grouped with fields such as palmistry and astrology in bookshops and libraries. Graphology cannot foretell the future. It simply reveals something of the true nature of the writer.

HOW DOES IT WORK?

The principles of graphology are very simple. Everything on a page of handwriting – or missing from it – says something about the writer. It is like a jigsaw where all the pieces fit togther but have a hidden message as well as a revealed image.

Many of the deductions made in handwriting analysis are really commonsense. Think about how people behave at a party: some people love the noise and beat of music and spend most of their time dancing, enjoying the attention their actions attract. Others prefer to find somewhere quiet and talk with friends. We make judgements of character from this behaviour.

We could make similar judgements by looking at their handwriting. The showy, affectionate, active person will have large, flamboyant writing which demands your attention, together with other signs of an extrovert and active character. The quieter, more reflective soul will have smaller, probably neater and more controlled writing, with pointers to a slightly less exhibitionist personality.

Two of the most common things people say about handwriting are: 'I have two different styles of writing', and 'I can't read anything my doctor writes!'

Taking the first statement, it is true that some people have styles of writing which appear, on first sight, to be different. However closer examination usually reveals that the key character indicators are the same in both samples: the changes are merely cosmetic. Being more relaxed, and not feeling that what you are writing is of great significance, does affect the look of the writing – rather as if you have changed from a business suit to jeans and a T-shirt.

On the question of doctors' writing, it does seem to be true that many doctors have a particularly illegible script. There are two reasons for this. The first is doctors are usually under a lot of pressure and are carrying out the task as quickly as possible. They write in a hurry, and although this does not invariably lead to neglected letter forms, it can have an effect. The second, and more revealing point, is that illegible writing is subconsciously deliberate: the writer does not want everyone to be able to read it. Why? Well doctors, like lawyers and some other professionals, are in the secrets business. Part of their job involves knowing things but not letting on. This requirement has crept into their writing style.

A FEW GROUND RULES

This book will help you start to analyze handwriting. It will give you a basic grounding in a valuable skill. You must not abuse that skill and you must be careful to use graphology with respect. These simple rules should be followed by anyone interested in using the skill.

- Never make judgements from one indicator. Look for supporting evidence. If the trait is there, so will be the back-up evidence.
- Treat the information you find in strict confidence.
- If you find a person has certain weaknesses, inform them in a tactful way.
- Always remember that there are positive aspects to even the most negative trait. One man's 'constancy' is another's 'dullness', and equally what some may see as 'spontaneity' may be viewed by others as 'impulsiveness'.

Read this book carefully for its briefing on the basics of graphology, then follow the character analyses at the end. Then you can start making your own assessments!

INITIAL IMPRESSIONS AND THE THREE ZONES

This chapter guides you through looking at the initial impression of a writing sample, and how to assess margins, size, and the all-important three zones of handwriting.

INITIAL IMPRESSIONS

The first thing to do with any piece of writing you wish to analyze is take a long careful look at the page and the general impression the writing creates.

Is it neat and tidy, or messy? Is it easy to read? Does it flow smoothly and fluently across the page? Is it full of eccentricities and odd shapes? Whatever it is, you can be sure that the writer deliberately produced it in this form, even if the reasons are subconscious.

Many people protest 'I do all I can to make my writing neat, but it always turns out a mess.' They cannot contradict their true nature: they may wish they were perfectionists, super-organized and superb communicators, but if they are not, their handwriting will show their real self. It should be noted that messy writing does not necessarily indicate a 'messy' person: they may be highly adaptable and versatile, or hyperactive, for example.

After a while you will gain more confidence in making some tentative, outline judgements just from running your eye over the writing. The next step is to examine more objectively different aspects of the way the writing is presented.

Margins

Margins reveal the writer's social attitudes. They are

the most obvious element in presentation of writing, but few people are even conscious of what their 'natural margin' is.

Non-existent margins reveal someone keen to fill every part of life's canvas, possibly at the expense of involvement with anybody else. The writer may also be rather selfish and mean. Very wide margins all round suggest a person who feels surrounded and inhibited by life, and is wary of trying to escape their 'cage'.

A wide upper margin reveals a hesitancy to begin proceedings – emotionally or in business. It is a cautious approach, but also shows generosity.

A narrow upper margin is more abrupt and aggressive – no hesitation here. The writer is informal, direct and keen to get results. He or she may also be a bad listener, and be trying to avoid too many complications in life.

A wide left hand margin indicates a lack of caution, and eagerness to face the world. If the margin is narrow, the writer is less hasty and more inhibited. In many cases left-hand margins narrow or broaden down the page. This shows the overall direction the writer is taking in life: towards a more (narrowing margin), or less (broadening), cautious approach.

Wide right hand margins reveal a fear of the future, and a lack of social ability. If the margin is narrow, the opposite is true, and the writer may be very fond of physical exercise and the outdoor life.

A deep margin at the foot of the page indicates reserve, but the writer may be a good listener. A very shallow margin suggests a talkative, lively personality.

Size

The bigger the writing, the more emotional (which can mean sentimental or impulsive – or other traits which stem from emotions) is its author. Equally, the smaller the size of the overall text, the more perfectionist and inhibited is its writer, and the more they keep a tight hold on their emotions.

small

Small writing (total size from tops of tall letters to bottoms of dropping letters under 8mm) indicates a slightly withdrawn, often quite intelligent, person. If it is very legible, the writer is pedantic, intelligent, perhaps academic, with excellent powers of concentration, and has low self-esteem. If it is difficult to read, the writer is more independent, perhaps lacking in social skills – a 'difficult' person. In either case, the writer prefers life backstage to out in the glare of the lights.

medium

Medium sized writing (total size 8-10mm, with typical middle zone occupying 3mm) indicates someone who is fairly conventional, and has a healthy balance between heart and head.

large

Large writing (10 – 12mm,) suggests ambition,

generosity, a tendency towards exaggeration and a need for self-expression.

huge

Very large writing (bigger than 11.5mm) means watch out! This person is bordering on the obsessional, and will stop at nothing to get his or her own way, although he or she will probably switch to something new before the challenge is over. They

upper middle lower **bridge**

will encounter many adventures as they barge through life!

Flow
Look at how easily the writing has flowed from the pen. Does it have a smooth, relaxed rhythm? Or is it taut, highly controlled and tense? A careful look at the flow of the sample will allow you to make an assessment of the writer's overall state of mind, their general attitude and mood.

Easy going, calm people have relaxed, smooth writing – but it will not necessarily be legible and even, because those are indicators of other characteristics.

Tense, uptight people will also have this tendency revealed in the tight, rigid handwriting they produce. Again, they may appear in other respects to be very calm and relaxed, but once you get a feel for assessing the flow of the writing, you will be able to see through that.

THE THREE ZONES

Handwriting divides into three easily distinguishable areas: the upper zone (tops of letters 'b', 'd', 'f', 'h', 'k', 'l', and 't'); the middle zone, which is everything on the line, and particularly letters 'a', 'c', 'e', 'i', 'm', 'n', 'o', 'r', 's', 'u', 'v', 'w', 'x', 'z'; and finally the area below the line, the lower zone, comprising the tails of letters 'g', 'j', 'p', 'q', and 'y'.

Each of the zones has a different significance in graphology.

The upper zone is the world of the imagination, ambition, spirituality, and our view of the future.

The middle zone is where our social attitudes and aspects of our everyday life are revealed.

The lower zone takes us into the subconscious and the realm of emotions.

In theory a 'balanced', 'normal'and 'mature' character will have writing which shows a balance between all these areas, giving them a well-rounded, well balanced personality. However we are very prejudiced about what is 'normal', and if handwriting is strongly dominated by one or other of these zones, that does not necessarily indicate a crazed, abnormal character.

As always, look for confirmation elsewhere in the handwriting of any assessment you make here. If there are dominant and neglected zones, take a careful look at both – it is an easy trap to only examine the most obvious, dominant aspect of the handwriting.

The upper zone
We are in the world of ambition, speculation, imagination, of our dreams for the future. Look at the tops of the letters and assess their size in proportion to the rest of the sample. Are they larger or smaller?

ambitious

Large upper zone writing indicates a person who aims to go places. They are striving for something, perhaps a career, or possibly in a spiritual sense. If the zone is very tall, they spend a lot of time fantasizing about the future, and could be a bit of a day dreamer. Look at the slant in this zone to see if it is directed backwards (to some key, formative event in the past, or showing a great conscience) or forwards (aiming for great things in the future). There is more guidance on slant in the next chapter.

unambitious

A small upper zone suggests a lack of spiritual and intellectual aspiration. These people are not striving for any great improvements and are perhaps rather passive. They lack imagination and a vision of the future, but have a very down to earth viewpoint and practical skills.

The middle zone
The writer's true feelings about their self, and their adaptability, are on show in the middle zone. A

'normal' middle zone is about 3mm high – for the most accurate measurement go to the 'i's' and 'm's'. Look at it in proportion to the other zones. If this ego-revealing section is larger than the other zones, the person will be too full of him or herself to actually do anything!

confidence

A large middle zone reveals a great deal of self-confidence, perhaps at the expense of a balanced view of the world. These writers can be pushy, and self-centred.

unsociable

A small middle zone betrays a crippling lack of self-confidence, an inability to handle other people well and perhaps a lack of social skills. However the positive aspect to a small middle zone is great independence and the capacity for sound judgement – the writer will be astute, but will lack the confidence to act on his or her observations.

The lower zone
This is the most primitive area of handwriting, where our most basic drives – for survival, sex and money – are revealed. It is also the area which shows to what extent the writer will be able to implement their ideas, to follow through their plans.

lusty

A large lower zone indicates a materialistic character, eager for worldly benefits, and probably with a
very strong sex drive. This person has strong
instincts and emotional responses, which can over-
ride more considered thought.

lacking

A small lower zone suggests inhibition about sex
and an overall timidity about life. This person will
be rather hesitant and lacking in the drive that may
be required to achieve what the writer is aiming for.
This will lead to frustration and resentment.

Although as has been said, there is no such thing as
'normal' writing – just as there is no such thing as a
'normal' person – one point to look out for is
consistency and balance.

Whether the handwriting is large or small, consistency between the three zones indicates a person at
ease with their true self. They may be shy, outgoing,
independent or obsessional, but if the handwriting is
regular across the three zones, the writer is probably
aware that they have these characteristics. They are
therefore likely to have a fair degree of inner
strength derived from this self knowledge.

So, in this chapter we have learned how to begin
to make character assessments by looking at the
most general points about the shape of the page, the

image it has, and the internal balance of the handwriting. The next step is to make some more precise judgements by examining the actual handwriting in greater depth.

DIRECTIONS – LINE, SLANT AND SPACING

This chapter will take you through the implications of several key aspects of handwriting: slant, starting and ending strokes, connections, pressure, spacing, flow, and line direction. Each of these gives strong indications about particular aspects of the writer's character, and helps to build up a comprehensive range of information about them.

SLANT

The slant of handwriting can be to the left (backwards), upright, or to the right (forwards). Since the natural movement of handwriting is to the right across the page, some slants are harder to achieve than others.

So why do some people write with a marked rightward slant, while others have a script with leans backwards? As always with graphology, the answer lies in the subconscious, in hidden impulses we don't even realise we have.

The slant is a major clue to the outer being of the writer: it reveals the degree of extroversion or introversion of the writer. The traits described below will be present in proportion to the extent of the slant. So a very deeply angled left slant indicates a far more introverted person than someone with a slight backward slant. You will become familiar with judging the angle of slant and the judgments you can make from it.

Left slant writing leans backwards, back into yourself, or towards the past. Such writers are intro-

backwards.

verted, self-conscious, perhaps still under a heavy influence of their childhood. They may desire protection, and can be unwilling to compromise, but they can also be very creative. They can be very strong individuals, but rather distant and self-reliant.

upright

Upright writing (no slant) shows independence, self-reliance, and a high degree of control. If the writing is very rigid and upright, the writer is extremely controlled and may be unwilling to show emotion. A more relaxed upright slant suggests a balanced personality who is able to deal with a wide variety of situations and people.

forwards

A right slant is the mark of a sociable, active and extrovert character, forward looking, keen for new challenges and new people.

This kind of person can also be impulsive and self-seeking.

A varied slant indicates a moody, variable character, switching between sociability and shyness. A degree of emotional confusion and disturbance is apparent, but this may be channelled positively into adaptability and versatility.

When considering slant, always look carefully to see if the overall slant is consistent throughout the script. You may find, for example, tell-tale signs of left slants with an eye on the past holding back a dynamic right slant.

STARTING STROKES

These are lines or arcs leading up to the first letter in many, but not all, of the words in the sample. They are good indicators of personal attitudes.

anchor

Anchor strokes curve up from the baseline to the letter. Such writers tend to lack maturity and confidence, and so are rather passive.

arc

An arc to the first letter of a word like this shows a rather self-satisfied and dogmatic character.

longer

Long starting strokes reveal someone who plans their next move carefully. However, the longer the stroke, the more they delay their action, so very long strokes betray time-wasting.

aggressive

Long, straight upstrokes beginning below the line

are a warning sign of aggression.

If there is *no starting stroke*, the writer enjoys 'hands on' experience, and getting on with the job as quickly as possible. They may also have an abrupt manner.

ENDING STROKES

These are the way words are finished off. They reveal the writer's social attitudes and qualities.

endstroke

Long endstrokes show generosity and social skills, an affinity with other people. If they are excessively long the writer is possessive and intolerant, trying to keep a hold on the people in their life. Long curling endstrokes reveal an imaginative, poetic trait.

rising

Rising endstrokes are a sign of someone who sets themselves very high standards, and can also indicate idealism and spirituality.

critical

A stroke that passes back through a letter or word illustrates a self-critical character, with a destructive element in their nature. If the stroke curves up and back without reaching the word it indicates a need for protection, and a sheltering from reality.

dramatic

Theatrical flourishes reflect the writer's social attitudes and behaviour in the obvious way!

Thread endings show intuition, nonchalance, and if they are downward, rebelliousness.

A lack of any ending strokes is the sign of a no nonsense, straightforward attitude to the job in hand: get it done and move on to the next job. Look elsewhere in the handwriting to see just how ruthless and abrupt this person is.

CONNECTING STROKES: THE FOUR STYLES OF HANDWRITING

There are four handwriting styles; garland, angular, arcade, and thread. Usually the handwriting is recognisably of one of these styles, but do keep an eye out for elements of the other styles to creep in.

Garland

Garland writing is rounded and flows well. It looks rather feminine (but is not necessarily by a female writer), and has the easy motion of a line of waves drawn on the page. It indicates a responsive, receptive , friendly and natural, kind personality who is perhaps easily led by others.

If the garlands are shallow and flat, the writer will be very impressionable, easy-going and with a tendency to thoughtlessness. Very deep garlands are the mark of massive lack of self-esteem and an easily dominated personality.

Arcade

Arcade writing is rather more contrived in execution, and features curves the other way up to garland writing – like writing a row of 'm's. It is found in writing by more formal, guarded people who are often very conscious of their own status. They are reserved, but can also have many practical skills.

Weak arcades, with barely recognisable curves, are a sign of deception, of a ruthless schemer.

Deep arcades distract attention from the letters in the writing: again, there is deception here, but of a more obvious, theatrical nature.

Angular

Angular writing is all straight lines and angles – no easy flow here. The writing is very rigid and controlled. An angular writer is aggressive, reluctant to compromise, and very determined: make sure this person is on your side!

Highly angular writing shows a great deal of aggression and mistrust.

Occasional angular strokes are fairly common, and reveal some kind of inner conflict, which may lead to bursts of aggression or sudden, ill-considered actions.

Thread

Thread writing weaves along at quite a pace, leaving few curves or elegant swoops in its path. It reveals a fast thinking, creative person perhaps lacking in sensuality and who can be very critical. They may also – like the writing – be rather evasive and difficult to pin down.

Thread writing is developed as the writer learns to simplify the writing process for speed. When executed well with legibility retained, it is a sign of an intelligent communicator. If it results in text which is difficult to read, the disorganised, impulsive side of the writer's nature is dominant.

When studying the connecting strokes, look out for the degree of connection between letters – few of us join up every letter we write in every word.

Less than five letters regularly connected: the writer is prone to stop during jobs to check on progress: this is fine, but if the job had been thought through properly in the first place, such pauses would not be necessary. Not a good planner, this person relies on intuition to get them by.

Connecting more than five letters indicates a more thorough, logical brain. If the connections extend between words, the writer is a fast, inventive thinker.

SPACING

Spacing between words and lines says much about the writer's closeness to people and to the extent of expression allowed for his or her emotions. The typical space left between words is roughly one wide letter across – about the space occupied by an 'm', for example.

Large spaces show someone who keeps other people at a distance, and can be aloof and stand-offish.

Regular spacing suggests good manners and social ability, it also indicates sound business sense.

Small spaces reveal a need to be with people, an enjoyment of their company and sometimes a lot of nervous energy. These people can be generous and kind, and are not good at being on their own.

A wide mix of different spacings is the mark of someone with an undisciplined, butterfly mind who cannot concentrate on one thing or one person for long. There may be some emotional confusion and a difficulty in sustaining relationships.

LINE DIRECTION

The underlying direction of the baseline (provided the sample is on unlined paper) shows the general drift of the writer's mind.

A rising baseline is being lifted by the hopes and aspirations of the writer, going upwards to a brighter, better future.

A steep rising baseline is the mark of an irrepressible character!

A falling baseline is caused by the unconscious mind pulling the spirits of the writer down, bringing worries about the present and doubts about the future, making them depressed and uncooperative.

An uneven line indicates nervousness and instability, and a rigidly even line is also a danger sign, as it shows a concentration on self-control and an over concern with what people might think of the writer, which means that the writer may have difficulty in expressing feelings.

PRESSURE

Pressure is dealt with more fully in the chapter on handwriting and health, as it is often an indicator of stress or illness. Pressure can be heavy, medium or light, and can be judged by feeling the underside of the paper, and simply looking at the impression the pen has made on the paper surface.

heavy

Heavy pressure shows vitality, energy, forcefulness and a 'live for today' mentality. The heavy writer is confident, noisy and can be domineering. He or she may also be clumsy.

Very heavy pressure indicates there is a lot of aggression in the writer.

medium

Medium pressure suggests adaptability, balance and friendliness in the writer. This denotes someone who is fairly relaxed about themselves and has a good self-knowledge.

light

Light pressure suggests weakness, sensitivity, and a tendency towards self-criticism. Such writers can be idealistic, dreamy, and creative, but they share one key characteristic: they are – literally – frightened to make their mark in the world.

SPEED

Assess the speed of writing, and you learn a lot about the writer's speed of thought, how fast they think and talk, how urgent their impulses are. It is not always easy to assess speed. Try tracing a pen over the writing to get a feel for how it was written. Look also for these signs:

Fast writing has smooth, simplified strokes, with dots turned into dashes in the rush to get them on the page. Such writers are confident, spontaneous, and eager to take the initiative. On the down side, they may be impetuous and lacking in judgment.

Regular speed writing is controlled, organised, and calm. The same applies to its writers.

Slow writing can be spotted by a narrowing left margin, very precise dots and bars, shaky loops, and some changes of direction. The writer is self-conscious, thoughtful, and may be slow to react in thought and emotions.

From this chapter it is clear that a good graphologist has to balance a number of complex and perhaps at first glance contradictory pieces of evidence before making firm character assessments.

For example a backward slanting, small script – which suggests a shy, introverted person – may be written very fast with medium pressure. This would indicate that the writer has the capacity to be quite responsive and friendly. The likelihood is that they have all these characteristics but that the more sociable aspects take time to emerge.

Always look for supporting evidence for your assessments, and be prepared for things that do not quite match up. These apparent contradictions will lead you to amuch better and fuller knowledge and understanding of the foibles and hidden depths of the writer. Personality is complicated cocktail of different elements, and handwriting reflects this.

Now that you are able to find out a lot from the general look of the handwriting, the next step is to examine individual letters to continue the journey into the writer's psyche.

FIVE KEY LETTERS

Although, as has been explained, it is important to consider all aspects of the handwriting when analyzing it, some letters are of particular significance. They hold the clues to some of the writer's deepest secrets.

In this chapter we take a long, hard look at the many variations of writing the letters 'd', 'i', 'g', 'I' and 't' – 'digit' – and their meaning. These letters cover some of the key areas in handwriting – the three zones, and capital letters.

The letter 'd' tells us much about the writer's social behaviour. The small 'i', and especially the 'i' dot, reveals many personal characteristics, while letter 'g' (or if necessary 'y'), with its drop below the line, tells us a lot about the writer's view of sex. The capital 'I' holds many clues to our central identity, and how we see ourselves. The letter 't' reveals much about the writer's sense of purpose and view of the future.

When you have identified traits from these letters, check for consistency of style with other, similar letters covering the same zones.

THE LETTER 'd'

d

Tall stem – an idealist, independant and high minded.If the stem is very tall: a day dreamer.

d

Short stem – humble, clever, lacking in imagination.

Wide loop – vain, tendency to be highly emotional. The wider the loop, the greater the importance placed on emotions, but also, the more open minded the writer is. The higher the loop, the greater the self-admiration. If the loop is narrow, some emotional repression is indicated.

d

Spread stem – an inflated view of the writer's own abilities. Very difficult person to work with!

d

Stem extends below base line – inflexible, tenacious.

d

Open at base – obstinate, a troublemaker.

d

Open at top – talkative.

THE SMALL 'i'

The 'i' dot is usually written in after the complete word has been formed, so it is marked in a hurry, with the pen eager to move off to write the next word. Yet most writers are extremely consistent in their 'i' dot placement.

Dot to left – caution, strong links with the past.

Dot to right – impatient, impulsive.

Low dot – good powers of concentration, accuracy.

High dot – enthusiasm for new ideas.

Dot below stem – repressed.

Circle dot – attention seeking, wants to give impression of sophistication, also lack of aggression.

$\overline{\iota}$

Dash dot – short tempered, hasty.

ι

Weak dot – sensitive, perhaps weak willed.

it

Dot linked to next letter – this is unusual and displays a clever, quick thinking mind.

ι

No dot – inattention to detail, non conformist, unconventional, independent.

ι

Arrow shaped – aggressive, can be cruel tongued. Variations of angled dots also show a tendency to be quick witted and sometimes rather nasty.

ι

Vertical dot – extremely critical.

Tick dot – ambition, desire to be rewarded.

Dot open to right – keen observer.
Varying dots – mood variation, need for constant change.

THE LETTER 'g'

The tail of the 'g', like 'j' and 'y', takes us into the primitive drives. When looking for the writer's attitude to sex, and material values, this is the place to start.

Deep, wide curve – love of romance, comtemplative.

Narrow, wide curve – unfulfilled, and perhaps very close to mother.

Deep loop – very active sexually very 'physical', probably very sporty.

g

Deep, open loop – frustrated, perhaps because the desires are unrealistic.

g

Deep, wide loop – quick to get involved, materialist.

g

Narrow, unfinished loop – fear of sex.

g

Narrow, completed loop – sexually repressed, lonely.

q

Short downstroke – sexually immature.

q

Long downstroke – 'reactive', dependent on others.

g

Triangular loop, *crossing stem* – watch out! Rules the roost, uncompromising.

g

Arc to left – avoids responsibility.

g

Rising endstroke – takes the initiative.

g

Falling endstroke – disappointment in sex or money.

g

Low crossing loop – sexually disappointed.

g

Short loop – very low sex drive.

THE CAPITAL 'I'

The capital 'I' shows how you see yourself: it is your own private image of what you think of your personality – your ego. Only in English is the personal pronoun a single letter. Graphologists in non English speaking countries do not place the same key emphasis on this letter.

The size of this letter in relation to the rest of the script is crucial. Larger 'I's indicate pride and self-confidence, smaller 'I's show a lack of self-esteem and a poor self-image. If the 'I' fits in with the standard capital letter size, the writer fits in well with other people. If there are large spaces between the 'I' and other letters and words, the writer is isolated, in a world apart.

Straight line – straightforward, genuine, concise.

Bars top and bottom – confident, clear thinking, well balanced.

Bars not linked to stem – inconsistent, insecure.

Small 'i' – immature, lacking confidence.

Small, cramped – insecure, self-conscious.

Tall, with deep, thin loop – need for status, tendency towards timidity.

Retraced stem – obsessive.

Knotted – selfish.

Curved, enclosed – defensive, vulnerable.

Small loop at top – helpful, down to earth.

Large loop at top – self-important.

Angular – good organiser, can be aggressive.

Large, over-inflated, exaggerated – reflects the ego!

Adjusted – unhappy, ill at ease.

Tick at top – concise, clear minded.

Falls below baseline -- deceitful, lack of honesty.

Looping to left in unusual way – possibly homosexual.

THE LETTER 't'

The letter 't' tells the graphologist a lot about the writer's drive and whether they will achieve their aims.

Low bar – feels inferior, lack of drive.

Middling bar – careful, conscientious, conservative.

High bar – ambitious, lots of willpower, imaginative.

Bar longer to left – cautious, strong sense of the past.

Bar longer to right – quick thinking, dislikes restrictions.

Short bar – restrained, cautious.

Long bar – energetic, eager to progress.

Tick down on left side – likely to take offence, tenacious.

Tick down on right – sarcastic, can be cruel.

Looped stem – sensitive, needs support.

Loop on bar – pride in achievements.

Cross through double 't' – very protective, strong nesting instinct.

Rising bar – enthusiasm, impulsive, high ambitions.

Falling bar – quick temper, unhappy.

Undulating bar – sociable, sense of humour

One point that should be stressed is that when examining individual letters, never make a judgement from just one example of a letter. I find it easiest to circle all the key letters and then go through all the d's, i's and so on to see what the typical letter formation is. If the shapes are different every time, draw your own conclusions about the writer's consistency of thought and action!

This chapter concludes the general notes on the basics of graphology. These notes have been written to make it easy for you to re-read the text on certain elements of handwriting analysis, to help you make a thorough character analysis efficiently and accurately. The next chapter looks at hints about the writer's health that can be gathered from graphology.

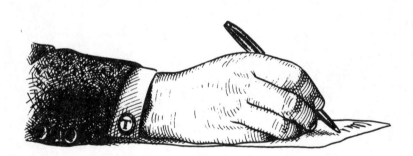

WRITING AND HEALTH

How can handwriting give any clues to the writer's health? It may sound crazy but the principle is very simple. Illness occurs in the body, and the body reacts as soon as the threat of illness appears - often well before our brains recognise the problem and warn us to visit the doctor.

Handwriting is carried out by the body, using instructions from the brain. But handwriting is almost a subconscious activity: we are thinking about what we are writing, not how we do it. So the process of writing in effect bypasses the conscious part of the brain, and the way that we write can reveal the state of the body, and any problems with it, before the brain realises that the body may be ill.

It must be emphasized that graphology can only indicate the possibility of illness, and certainly not diagnose it. If you spot any signs of illness in writing you are analyzing, you should suggest that the writer has a check up or visits their doctor.

Graphology is perhaps most useful in spotting the disease of modern times: stress. Stress creeps up on people and very often the first they are aware of the problem is when they are severely fatigued or upset. It is often initially manifested by fatigue, the body's own safety valve, which creeps up on the sufferer very slowly.

One of the best tools a graphologist has in spotting stress is assessing the pressure of the handwriting.

PRESSURE

The simplest way to measure the pressure used to make the handwriting sample is to feel the underside of the paper. Your fingertips will sense how firmly the pen or pencil was applied to the paper.

weak

Light pressure can indicate a lack of strength in the writer, a weakness perhaps brought about by the body devoting its energies elsewhere to fight illness.

variable

Variable pressure is the sign of a writer who is losing strength, but fighting back, trying not to give up the struggle. An 'i' dot that is lighter than the stem of the letter can indicate this.

Very heavy

Very heavy pressure is a warning sign that the writer is under a lot of stress, and that this stress is being held inside, unable to find a way out. Particularly heavy 'i' dots are a sign of acute frustration.

Other danger signals of stress in handwriting include the following:

- Large, uncharacteristic gaps between individual letters or words, perhaps only occurring spasmodically.
- Poor line spacing, which tends to show emotional instability, anxiety, and desperation.
- Variations in slant which reveal anxiety.
- A descending baseline, which suggests depression

and tiredness.

- Threads in the middle of words, which show that inner resources are stretched, but that the writer is trying to keep up appearances.
- An uneven left hand margin, which denotes inner turmoil.
- The sudden appearance of capital letters in the middle of words, which shows extreme anxiety.

- A triangular 'T' bar, or a 'T' with an acutely downward facing bar. Both show uncertainty and depression.

- Drooping connecting or end strokes, which show depression and fatigue.
- Lines that look like a series of descending steps show that stamina is being worn down.
- Fading writing is a sign of fatigue.
- Dots may appear at the end of words. These are points where the hand took a momentary rest – a warning of fatigue.
- Breaks in the rhythm of the writing, revealed by sudden lurches within letters, also indicate stress.
- A dimished lower zone can indicate trauma and lack of drive.

Other elements to look out for when assessing the health of the writer include any broken loops or hooks in the writing, as these can show a hidden ailment.

● A spot on the top loop of letters such as 'h' or 'k' can indicate eye strain or headaches.

● A spot on the base of, or halfway up the loop of a 'g', 'j' or 'y' can indicate a foot or knee problem.

● A bent opening stroke to a letter may signal a back ailment of some kind.
● Amendments and retouching can show anxiety.
● Fluctuation of heavy to light pressure, may indicate the writer is asthmatic.
● Weak 't' bars and weak lower loops hint at lung trouble.
● Varying line direction could be a sign of liver trouble.
● Frequent underlinings and other irregularities are a sign of paranoia.
● A gap after a first letter suggests a speech defect.

One point to bear in mind when looking at the writer's health through their handwriting is that alcohol and some other drugs do have an effect on the script, in a way that physical disability does not.

The writer who has been drinking heavily will produce a varied, less consistent script, with taller and wider letters, variable pressure, and less defined strokes.

Anti depressant drugs can slow down reaction and reduce handwriting fluency too.

Again it should be emphasized that any conclusions you draw in this sensitive area should be treated with caution and respect.

CHILDREN'S WRITING

The development of a child's writing from a mere copying exercise to using words as a vehicle for expression is one of the most exciting aspects of childhood.

From their early efforts, erratic and faltering, through the impressionable early teens, to their adulthood, children's writing changes. It moves from the apeing of the copybook to an individual style with its own mechanical efficiency, from a conscious to a subconscious process, and charts the child's development on the way.

Graphology can help a parent monitor a child's intellectual and emotional development, to spot danger signs of anxiety, and to detect the common tendency for children to try out different writing styles before assimilating them into their own natural handwriting, just as they imitate other people's behaviour during their impressionable years.

STAGES IN DEVELOPMENT

The typical stages of development in a child's handwriting are outlined below. The age ranges given are approximate and all children develop in different ways, so these must be seen as broad generalisations. They still provide valuable guidance on the handwriting development process.

Age 5-7. The child is taught to copy individual letters, and inevitably mimics the style as well as the shape of the letters in the example.

Age 8-10. Handwriting has become more automatic and individual touches start to appear. The child is encouraged to link the letters of words together – 'joined up writing'. Once achieved, children often see this as a sign of sophistication, but in the meantime, and for quite a long period, they will carry on printing letters because the overall effect is neater.

Age 10-12. Writing is now a natural process, and content occupies more of the conscious brain than the mechanics of how the writing is achieved. However neatness and legibility are commented on by parents and teachers alike, and the child will carry over an increased awareness of presentation in the writing. Simplifications start to appear (ommitting loops for example) as the hand and brain learn short cuts in forming letters.

Age 13-17. The image of handwriting increases in significance for the writer. Deliberate stylistic changes will be made, usually not being retained longer than two years. These are a symptom of the stage of experimentation and imitation of others, and (in the later teens) an urge to show more individuality.

During puberty the sudden and uncontrollable surges of emotions which children experience is reflected in bursts of heavy pressure. After this, it is common in adolescence for the child to write with a much lighter pressure for a period of up to two years. This shows a time of lack of confidence and insecurity concerning their identity. It is also quite common for a teenager to switch to backward slanted handwriting for a while. This reflects a great awareness of self-image and a wish to appear adult and sophisticated.

LEGIBILITY

Adults have the luxury of opting to use a typewriter

or word processor for written communication if their handwriting is difficult for others to read. Children do not, in the main, have such a choice, and the importance of legibility in their handwriting cannot be underplayed.

From their first copied line of letters, through all their school examinations, to their letters applying for jobs, the vital aspect of a child's writing is that people can read it easily. Many teachers privately admit that poorly presented work, whatever its true quality, is likely to be marked more harshly than work which is easy to read.

A lot of pressure is applied to children with illegible writing to improve it. This applies particularly to girls, who are generally expected to have neater handwriting than boys. There is no reason why this should be so, indeed the graphologist cannot tell the sex of the writer from a sample of handwriting.

It must be understood that illegible writing by children can have a variety of causes, but is most unlikely to be a result of poor writing technique: the causes will lie much deeper. Some typical reasons for illegible writing in children are listed here.

1 Consistently very illegible writing is a sign of deep emotional problems, causing repression and anxiety.

2 The natural stage of simplifying writing style for efficiency – a sign of high intelligence – can be over executed, creating neglected letter forms.

3 Lack of concentration can lead to the child 'forgetting' to ensure their writing can be easily read. They do not have the capacity to keep their attention on the job in hand. Wildly undulating baselines are another symptom of this.

4 Fear of failure. Children under massive pressure to succeed are under stress, and illegible writing

can be a defensive measure to protect the child from blame for poor content in their work – it creates an excuse for bad marks.

Understandably, parents become very concerned if their child's writing is unreadable. One initial practical step is to equip the child with a fibre tip pen. These flow more easily across the page and are a smoother writing implement.

However, it is likely there is a subconscious reason for the lack of expression the child is showing through illegible writing. Parents should consider whether the child is unhappy in some way, or perhaps simply bored with what they are doing. Never force a child to change their handwriting style in a bid for greater legibility. You will be storing up problems for the future, by repressing some aspect of the child's character.

SIGNS OF ANXIETY

No-one likes to think of their child as suffering from anxiety, but children do go through stages of stress, as the body changes, as emotions develop, during exams, etc. The signs of anxiety listed here should cause concern only if they last for an extended period.

- Rigid, restrained writing, with a significant lack of curves. Shows tension, and can indicate a deliberate holding back, perhaps refusing to live up to the expectations of parents.
- Repeated heavy amendments. Show great sensitivity to criticism and a fear of failure.
- Reversing letters. The mark of poor concentration, possibly caused by anxiety. Can also be a symptom of dyslexia.
- Narrowing of letter widths. Anxiety.
- Extra large handwriting during the years of puberty. The writing is compensating for feelings

of inferiority.

- Columning of words, when the writing reads as usual across the page but words are carefully placed in line with words above them on the page. This shows a fear of authority and an attempt to meet the demands of conformity.
- Again, whenever these traits are apparent for long periods, look for the underlying cause: do not cure the symptom, look for the hidden problem.

SIMPLIFICATION AND EMBELLISHMENT

These apparently contradictory actions are signs of character development, and are very easy to spot.

Simplification involves the dropping of parts of letter forms without compromising readability, to achieve rapid, efficient and often elegant writing. This is a sign of intelligence and is particularly significant if it appears before the age of nine.

Another sign of early intelligence is upright, unslanted writing, which indicates an old head on young shoulders.

Embellishment is the addition of flourishes to the writing in an attempt to give it a unique and distinctive image. It shows a wish to be recognised and appreciated, and a step away from the conformity of the copybook style to something with more individualism. The embellishments will be dropped or adapted to form part of the writer's adult handwriting style.

THE LEFT HANDED CHILD

About a fifth of all people are left handed. Some of them experience difficulty in writing because the act of pushing a pen across the page – as opposed to the pulling motion used by the right handed writer – causes them problems.

The left hander has to adapt and hold the pen in a different way to write across the page, and some end up with a very contorted pose in their efforts to achieve this. Provided this does not cause physical pain or affect the handwriting , it does not matter how the left hander solves the problem. Some sensible suggestions include placing the writing paper slightly to the left, to give the arm more room to move in to; and ensuring that the pen or pencil is gripped at least 3cm from the tip, so that words already written are not smudged or concealed by the moving hand.

Using this sensible advice, the left handed writer should suffer no disadvantage in how they write – you cannot spot them from their handwriting style. As is now well known, the worst thing you can do is force them to hold the pen in their right hand, because this repression inflicts deep pyschological suffering.

EXAMPLES

but they don t live
to me. I am Eight
My birthday is on
th. I was born in

Girl age eight
Typical writing of an eight year old. Letters are

printed with frequent lapses in size discipline. The consistent medium pressure is a healthy sign that there are no great anxieties lurking under the surface.

When I get up on Easter mornin to the living room and look at of them and at bedtime I have morning I eat some more.

Boy age 10

Some letters are joined together in this script, showing an increase in speed of writing. A slight right slant has crept in, and the 'I' has been simplified into a straight line. This suggests growing independence and an extrovert nature. The broadening margin shows that this chap is always keen to get going on the next task. You will notice the letter 't', is significantly shorter than other letters. This letter is identified with drive, and it would usually be assumed that this boy does not at present have a great deal of application and ambition. Apparently at his school, small 't's are taught as part of handwriting style.

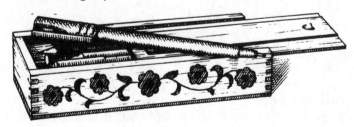

My hobbies are Badminton, Swimming Badminton. I Like badminton because at my old school in Ramsbottom. I little tournament between all of the

to Like it so I started to go to the The following year I went to Badminton

Boy age 10
This writing has excellent form and proportion, and, like the other 10-year-old, a few of the letters have been connected. The capital 'B' shaped like the number 13 suggests an interest in mathematics, and the fully completed lower loops show a well developed imagination. Margin discipline is strong, indicating a healthy attitude to the world around him, and the slight left slant, combined with the conventional capital 'I', reveals shyness and a wish to conform.

In the holidays me and my and ▇ Sometimes we play Foot Most holidays we go to ingold Or we just go For daytrips In the rest of our sparetime

Age 15
Although five years older, this child's writing is very

similar in development to the previous example. This indicates a lack of maturity. The heavy pressure suggests some form of anxiety, and there have been frequent hesitations during writing what is a rather slow script.

in which the process of writ unique individual characteristics. text will help his study, and I look forward to reading out on my handwriting and will look once it is completed.

Girl 14

This writing is very neat and legible, well disciplined, and completely connected. This suggests a balanced character with a very clear thinking mind. The slight left slant, when considered with the wide gaps between words, shows that the writer keeps her emotions to herself: she is not ostentatious. The wide left margin indicates that she is keen to face the future but these other signs suggests that at times she holds herself back. Some starting strokes are also evident, which backs up the suggestion of a cautious approach to life. The open loops show that this is not due to inhibition or repression.

Sean Callery is writing a
in which he endeavours
characters from a variety
to include all kinds of
how handwriting develops
through to one in which

Girl 16
This is an elegant script with a right slant. The
writer is outgoing and sociable, but the deep backward loops show a close relationship with a parent.
Inner loops on the 'o's show some secrecy, and the
varying positions of the 'i dots' indicate a need for
change and excitement.

A general point when examining the handwriting of
a child is that, in the end, content is much more
important than appearance. A happy, imaginative,
confident child may have writing that is difficult to
read, but if the mind develops well they will learn in
time the value of expressing themselves in the
written word.
It is relatively easy, by careful training or by
switching to another writing format such as a
typewriter, to get legible words onto a page. The
child should be judged by what these words express
rather than how they are applied to a sheet of paper.
So even if your child has wildly illegible handwrit-

ing, provided you are sure that this is not cause by lurking emotional or mental trauma, do keep the 'problem' in proportion. Where graphology can help is in identifying possible hidden unhappiness and, hopefully, monitoring its demise.

INSIDE THE SIGNATURE

Your signature is unique. It is also your public face. It represents you on important documents, on messages to friends: it is your mark of promise, your bond. And it says more about you than any other set of letters.

The signature is a multi-purpose sign. It commits you to, say, repay a debt, that what you state on your tax form is correct, that you support the views expressed in a letter – it is used to help enforce the law. Yet it is also used in personal communication to friends, wishing someone a happy birthday, and much more.

So it is not surprising that people use variations of their signatures depending on what it is being used for. A signature on a legal document might be signed with your full name, including initial letters of middle names. A letter to a friend might simply be signed with a pet name.

Your signature is central to your identity, yet you sign your name thousands of times in your life, so often that writing it becomes a completely automatic, mechanical act. The signature is a stylized form of writing: it shows how you want the world to percieve you.

As always in graphology, the rules of common-sense apply. Ask the writer to produce their typical signature that they would use to sign a cheque. Use that for your analysis.

The first thing to consider with the signature is how it compares with the rest of the person's handwriting. Although signatures tend to be slightly stylized, they echo traits in the script. Any differences between the two show a discrepancy between the writer's view of their own character and how they expect to be regarded – there is something false here. The meaning of the differences is explained in each section of this chapter.

SIZE

The larger the signature, the greater the writer's self esteem, and expectation that this should be recognised.

Large signature: this shows a sense of high status – which may in real life be the case, but in terms of the signature that is not the point – of having value.

If the signature is larger than the handwriting, the writer carries a pretence of higher self esteem – and confidence – than is the case. It is a 'front'.

Medium size signature (same as handwriting): shows a balance of sense of value and modesty. If it is the same size as the script it shows someone with a knowledge of, and acceptance of, how he or she is perceived. When this person is in public, they do not put on an act.

Small signature: the writer expects little esteem from other people. This may imply a high degree of self-motivation and disregard for what people think, but is more likely to be a sign of low self-confidence.

If the signature is smaller than the script, the writer does not expect recognition of their worth. It may be this is a deliberate holding back, a defensive posture.

CONTENT

For typical use, the majority of people nowadays use their full first name and surname. Those who choose not to and opt for use of initials instead of their christian name(s) will have one of two reasons:

a) They prefer the formality and reserve of the more 'businesslike' initials, in which case they are likely to have conventional, perhaps even old fashioned, values, or
b) they deeply dislike their first name.

Writing your full name in your signature reveals a more informal, relaxed approach to life – the writer likes to get on first name terms quickly.

LEGIBILITY

As has been noted elsewhere in this book, legibility bears little relation to speed: the fast writer can still be perfectly readable, and the slow writer can have an impossibly messy script. In handwriting, legibility is, subconsciously, a matter of choice. The same applies in the signature.

If the illegible signature closes a business letter, it shows that the writer does not consider their name to be of great importance to the matter in hand: they are a mere functionary. The personal signature may be very different.

A consistently illegible signature implies that 'you really ought to know who I am, and if you don't, it is your loss!'. A certain arrogance and self importance is apparent.

If the surname is more legible than the first name the writer shows reserve on first contact with people – a holding back of familiarity until they get to know a person better.

A first name more legible than the surname reveals a more approachable, direct person who will make a great effort to be friendly.

Complete legibility shows open and straightforward social attitudes. The writer is happy to be accepted as they are.

COMPARISONS ON LEGIBILITY WITH SCRIPT

Legible script, illegible signature: the writer feels what is said is of more importance than his or her true identity, and is hiding his or her true self.

Illegible script, illegible signature: a deliberate attempt to create an aura of mystery and enigma around the writer, who enjoys the idea of being difficult to know. They do not want you to know what they are really thinking!

Illegible script, legible signature: greater importance placed on the writer's name than on what they actually say. Draw the obvious conclusion!

PLACEMENT

Like the margins and layout of the page, placement of signature is quite revealing. Business letters should not be used for analysis as they have a standard format.

Signature on left: writer seems in public to be withdrawing from the future, clinging to the past. May be a pose.

Signature in the middle: a show of importance, a need for attention.

Signature on right: forward looking, natural.

DIRECTION AND SLANT

The same interpretations on line direction and slant are made as for the script, but watch out for differences between the signature and the handwriting.

Signature rising more than handwriting: the writer is showing their optimism and energy to the outside world, but some of this is just show. The reality, revealed in the less image-conscious handwriting, is a more balanced, level headed approach.

Signature falls more than handwriting: the same principle reveals an appearance of pessimism and lack of vitality that may not be an accurate reflection of the writer's true feelings.

Right slant signature: an outgoing, bubbly, outer persona.

Left slant signature: does not push self forward.

EMBELLISHMENTS

The signature stands in its own right. Any additional strokes are a deliberate attempt to draw more attention to it.

Lines through signature: self-critical, unhappy.

Underlining: need for responsibility and importance. Betrays a lack of self-confidence and a need for recognition and status.

Circles: wants to be protected. May be very defensive and needs reasssurance.

Full stop: a sign of self-centredness – 'the world stops with me'!

Vertical line at end: a block on the outside world, this person has a private world to retreat into.

Larger letters or names: irregularities in letter or name size within the signature draw attention to certain parts of it, stressing their importance to the writer. Typically, formal people increase the size of the surname, for example.

EXAMPLES

Helen Knightley

This is a straightforward, unembellished signature, in the garland style. The impression is one of openness, (reinforced by the open top to the 'g'), softness, and the deep lower loop suggests a strong pull to family.

Marian Head

The initial capitals are the same size as the rest of the letters, indicating an informal, easy-going social image. The diminished upper zone shows self-sufficiency. The letters have angled tops and curving bases, revealing a gentle nature and a sharp mind. The double loops inside the 'a's indicate great secrecy: this person is very capable socially, but highly self-reliant and does not let people know her inner thoughts very frequently.

An interesting point about this signature is that only

part of it - the surname – is underlined. This emphasizes the importance of the surname, yet the letters of the first name are disproportionately large. This person has two images: a formal, businesslike, professional manner, and a more chatty and extrovert private nature.

This signature starts with a flamboyant gesture and ends with a series of decreasing letter sizes and a long, looped underline embellishment. This person likes to make a big, stylish entrance to make his presence felt, but after this he retreats from this showy manner. The underline stresses his importance and status (see how it accentuates his first name again – the manner is informal). The crucifix like 't' suggests an interest in religion.

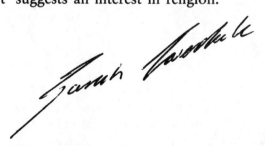

This signature has a very steep rise, showing masses

of vitality and optimism. The image is carefully calculated, however: look at the initial pause before commencing quite a long starting stroke. The public image of liveliness and energy is carefully prepared. In fact in this case the signature is very different to the handwriting, which has a much more down to earth, steady baseline, confirming the impression that this person likes to make an lively impression.

Again a rising signature which suggests a bubbly, optimistic manner. This person is very sociable in public, but see how the first name is neglected down to a single letter with a line through it. This person does not reveal their true self in public.

The use of both initials, complete with full stops, shows reserve and a pedantic manner. Yet in the surname is a huge embellished loop, twice the size of the other letters, ending in a rising stroke. Everything happens underneath the surface with this person! There is a great hidden sensual world in here. Note the self-critical dash 'i' dot, too.

The first letters of each name are far larger than the rest of this indecipherable signature. The large, narrow initial letters show a high self-regard combined with shyness. This indication of reserve is reinforced by the illegible name – this person is not easy to get to know and is very independent.

There is a great deal of controlled aggression here in the deep, heavy pressure vertical lines. The large circle at the start of the surname is a protective, defensive measure hiding insecurities. The angled 'i' dot indicates a liking for sarcasm, and the tall starting stroke on the 'p' is a classic sign of stubbornness.

The sweeping, drooping line through the surname is a sign of great self-criticism in professional life. The large curve of the initial 'g' letter is protecting the rest of the first name, and the large underlining stroke steers clear of the christian name. It all adds up to someone who regards their private and professional lives as entirely separate existences.

A highly embellished signature which only comprises the christian name. The circle 'i' dots show a strong desire to be seen as sophisticated. The heavy rising underline shows a high view of self worth, and the stylized 'kiss' crosses indicate an extravagantly showy image. The dots before and after the name imply that this image has been carefully planned and executed. This person wants to be seen as a 'star', and is prepared to work hard at it!

You are now equipped to gain some very deep understandings of what a person is really like from their handwriting, and, from their signature, how they would like to be seen. It is rare for there to be no discrepancy at all between script and signature style, and the differences are usually very revealing. Study them carefully, and always bear in mind the essential differences between the role of handwriting – to communicate information – and the signature – to say who you are.

TWENTY QUESTIONS AND SOME INDIVIDUAL CHARACTER TRAITS

Although it is possible to perform a character analysis from handwriting without even checking over the individual letters, there are some character traits which are indicated by specific elements in the handwriting.

This chapter begins with a set of twenty of the commonest questions you are likely to ask about the person's character, and tells you where to look in the handwriting for the answers. It then provides an extensive list of notable idiosyncracies in writing and what they mean.

1 How strong is your sex drive?
Indications of a high sex drive include: right slant; large upper and lower zone (look for deep loops on tails of letters); saucer shaped 't' bars (indulgence) or 't' bars well above stem (imagination); inflated stems to 'p's; heavy pressure; tight spacing; thick strokes, and rising strokes to the right. A variety of different lower zone formations implies a variety of partners or of sexual activity – possibly bi-sexual tendencies. If the writing is 'all over the place', there may be a distinct immorality.

Low sex drive can be identified by: left slant; narrow, short loops to tails; light pressure; wide spacing; knotted or enclosed 'a's and 'o's; narrow writing in a garland formation.

2 Are you a romantic?
Romantic writing will feature; a marked slant, right

or left; medium pressure; full middle zone and tall upper zone; wide, inflated loops in any zone.

Lack of romanticism is shown by upright, controlled writing with a limited upper zone; tight loops; and angular script.

3 Are you self-confident?

Confidence is indicated by: large, broad writing; rising baseline; large capital 'I'; large loops on 'I's' and 'j's' (indicate a desire for responsibility); no starting strokes; long, straight, downstrokes; firm pressure; large middle zone.

Lack of confidence can be identified by: small, narrow writing; falling baseline; left slant; low or left sided 't' crosses; wide right hand margin; amendments; knotted 'a's and 'o's.

4 Are you intelligent?

For signs of intelligence look for: small to medium size script; short breaks between some letters in a word; 'i' dots linking to next letter; simplified formation; points on letters, especially 'm's and 'n's; 'v' formations in the writing show analytical ability.

Lack of intelligence is suggested by: childlike script with large middle zone; full but short loops on tails of letters; large gaps between letters.

5 Are you a leader?

For leadership qualities look out for: regular script; large size; neat layout; strong baseline; closed 'a' and 'o'; firm 't' cross.

Poor leadership potential is revealed by: small, narrow script; ornate capitals; endstrokes back into words; wide right margin; missing 'i' dots and 't' bars.

6 Are you well organised?

A good organiser will have: balanced layout with good spacing; clean margins; rounded tops to letters (shows a methodical mind); a very well proportioned 'f'; loops on upper zone; starting strokes.

Someone definately not to be left in charge of the office would have a messy, untidy script; many amended letters; a mixed slant; over-simplified text; and elaborate capital letters.

7 Are you honest?

Honesty is indicated by: right slanted, legible script; letters increase slightly in size at end of words; open 'a's, 'd's and 'o's. Dishonest writing will have a varying middle zone; extremes in slant and broadness of letters; letter forms open at baseline; endstrokes failing to reach the baseline; double walls or knots inside letters; circled 'i' dots; signature different to script.

8 Are you sociable?

For someone who is a good mixer, the signs are: narrow maragins; right slant; legible, broad script; open 'a's and 'o's and open base of capital 'B'; extended endstrokes; rounded lower zone loops; pointed tops to capital 'M'.

An unsociable writer will have: wide margins and spacing; left or upright slant; closed or knotted 'a's and 'o's.

9 Are you happy?

Obviously this applies to the person's general state of mind, and not the mood of the moment.

Happy and secure people will generally have an upright or right slanted script with a slightly rising baseline; full, rounded script with large capitals;

long, rounded loops; rising 't' bars and 'i' dots positioned up to the right.

Someone who is depressed will write spiky writing with varying pressure; a falling baseline and short, drooping endstrokes; low crossings of loops; wide spacing; differing proportions of letters; and perhaps a line through the signature.

10 Do you have a quick temper?
Bad temper is revealed by: angular writing with ticks on starting strokes and hooks on crossing strokes; mixed pressure (watch out if the pressure varies a lot – the writer is extremely temperamental); triangle shaped loops; thick or sharpened 't' bars. A more tolerant, even tempered person will have: straight left margin and baseline; threads at the ends of words or some long endstrokes; short 't' bars; rounded loops. Wavy lines in the script reveal a good sense of humour.

11 Are you a conformist?
The mark of the rigid conformist is a controlled script on an even baseline; a short upper zone, with a long lower zone if there is a strong practical streak; narrow spacing; very little embellishment.

A more unconventional, spirited writer will use unusual letter forms, perhaps mirror images of normal letters; wedge formations (like very broad points) show an independent thinker; a mixed slant, poor layout and missing or circled 'i' dots. Great versatility and adaptability is shown in a varied script, although this can indicate a lack of discipline.

12 Are you artistic?
Artistic writing usually features elegant embellishments, while some of the script is simplified; a tall upper zone and long loops; disconnected and origi-

nal letter forms; a wide left margin can show an appreciation of art.

The more technically oriented person will write in thin script, perhaps with a rather square, boxy look to it; the writing will be accurate and consistent, although not necessarily legible!

13 Are you ambitious?

Ambitious writing is fast, and generally has right slant tendencies and a rising baseline; rising 't' bars; an extended upper zone, deep, narrow loops, and a large capital 'I'.

Lack of ambition is shown by more restricted, left oriented writing with, in particular, a diminished upper zone; wide right margin; descending endstrokes.

14 Are you selfish?

Hooks and claws are the main tell-tale signs here. Look for: hooks on endstrokes and claws starting strokes; inward hooks; narrow margins; large capitals; heavy 't' bars; tight spacing.

A more generous, less self-centred person will have wider spaces between words, long endstrokes; a wide left margin.

15 Are you persuasive?

The good, persuasive salesman has legible but simplified writing; open 'o's, 'd's and 'a's, rounded script; narrow bottom margins; firm pressure; letters getting smaller towards the end of words; large capital letters.

Less persuasive character is shown be a more ornate script, with extreme, sometimes pointed loops; left slant; large breaks within words.

16 Are you impulsive?

The impulsive writer uses a fast, simplified script; size and spacing will vary; no loops; right slant; light pressure.

The more careful and cautious person has upright or left slants; narrow writing; starting strokes; breaks within words; leftward tendencies in 'i' dots and 't' bars; wide right margin.

17 Are you reliable?

The reliable writer has firm pressure, legible writing and signature; diminishing size toward the end of words; completed loops in lower zone; even left margin; closed 'a's, 'd's and 'o's.

Unreliability is revealed by an irregular baseline; wavy strokes; inconsistencies in pattern; middle zone open at baseline; breaks in words; weak 't' crosses.

18 Are you the outdoor type?

The outdoor type has firm pressure; long lower zone; lots of loops; broad script.

Someone who is less happy outdoors writes with a medium script with great accuracy; less pronounced loops.

19 Are you fussy?

Fussiness is quite easy to spot. Look for slow, legible writing with a neat layout; starting strokes; amendments; dominant middle zone; closed 'a's and 'o's.

For the opposite, there will be missing 'i' dots and 't' bars; lack of legibility; gaps between letters.

20 Are you an idealist?

The idealist, and often the very religious person, has a dominant upper zone; long rising endstrokes; full loops especially in the upper zone; high 't' crosses. A more down to earth and practical approach is indicated by starting strokes; balanced writing; low 't' crosses.

A number of ways of spotting character traits have been identified in other chapters, but the list below gives some other examples of features in writing and their meanings.

CLUE	MEANING
Legibility	sincere, careful
Illegibility	need for freedom, lack of control
Fast	quick thinking
Simplified writing	intelligence

Hooks in general are a sign of acquisitiveness for money, friends, knowledge, etc:

Hook at end of words	aggressive
Hook at start of words	avaricious
Downward hook on right	matter of fact, tenacious
Upward hook on right	greedy, envious
Downward hook on left	selfish, acquisitive
Upward hook on right	dry humour, down to earth

Capital letters

Large capitals	vain, assertive, imaginative
Same size as script	adaptable, fits in with others
Smaller than script	submissive
Narrow capitals and letters	shy, inhibited
Broad capitals and letters	extravagant, wasteful
Flourishes on capitals	conceited
Flourishes in general	flair
Embellished flourishes	showy

Overall style

Rigid writing	cautious, restrained
Neglected letter forms which are uneven or irregular	lack of control
Uneven	nervous
Thick writing	lack of sensuality
Garlands	amiable, easy going
Arcades	tactful
Angular	bad tempered, cruel
Heavy pressure angular	brutal, aggressive

Open letters	open, talkative
Open on right	talks about self
Open on right, looped	unable to keep a secret
Open on left	talks about others, gossips
Open at bottom	dishonest

Knots are generally a signal of some form of hesitation, and are interpreted as a deliberate pause to make some kind of adjustment. Many knots in the handwriting reveal a tenacious person who does not easily give up:

Knot on left (a)	deceives others
Knot on right (a)	deceives self
Knot on right (f)	secretive
Square letters	mechanical ability, calculating
Letters filled with ink	sensual
Unusual shapes above line	imaginative
Unusual shapes below the line	erotic
Wavy starting strokes	sense of humour

Loop at start of stroke	jealous: the smaller the loop, the more personal the reason
Arc at start of word	fixed opinions
Tick starting stroke	obstinate, petulant
Curled endstroke upwards(a)	pretentious
Endstroke rising	courageous, optimistic, has initiative
Endstroke rising to left	self-protective
Endstroke rising to right	day dreamer
Long endstroke (e)	generous
Long endstroke down to right	reserved, obstinacy
Loops ending in falling endstroke	sadness about money or sex
Threads at word endings	astute
Top bars long – heavy	domineering
Top bars long – rising	self-important, protective
Letters like numerals	interest in mathematics; craving for money, possessions

Pressure: heavy	energetic, forceful, noisy
Pressure: light	lacking emotional depth
Pointed tops to letters	penetrating mind
Pointed bottom to letters	uncompromising, greedy
Very pointed but narrow	defensive
Square letters	mechanical skill
Ink filled letters	sensual
Numerous amendments	high anxiety
Bar across top of word	protective, aiming to keep in control
Top bar above stem of letter	does not always achieve expectations, perhaps untrustworthy
Letters shaped like numbers	mathematical ability, materialism
Snaking, winding letter forms	devious
Overlapping strokes within letter	likes being in a tight clique

A STEP BY STEP GUIDE TO CHARACTER ANALYSIS

To carry out your analysis you need a typical sample of handwriting, with signature, on unlined paper.

You can then follow the processes outlined in the first three chapters of this book, examining the overall look, the layout and presentation, and finally the features of the individual letters and connections themselves. Look out for oddities and inconsistencies – they are revealing clues. I find it helpful to circle anything worth noting – a key letter, or a variation from the norm – in different coloured ink.

Note down the meaning of all the things you have found in the handwriting, and pay particular attention to any traits which you find repeatedly: these will be central to the writer's character. Be prepared for contradictions in your findings. You may realise you made a mistake, or that the contradictions are just part of the person's make-up. Try to be as objective as possible, especially if you have met the writer already: you should not impose your preconceptions on the analysis.

EXAMPLES

All these analyses were carried out fairly fast to achieve a quick thumbnail sketch of the writer's character. As you will see, even though the analysis was very fast, it still reveals many elements of character that a one hour meeting with the writer would not have shown up.

Airline meals — who
I'd prefer to take me own
Accustomed as I've beca
I believe that I've became
on airline meals.
The only one that will live
reasons positive is Air Indi
journey from London to Sy
universe was made bearable
was handed out every fiv
had taken off from yet a
Their excellent curries comp
nan bread and sambals we
up to.

Initial impressions: very legible, rounded letter forms
– clear thinker, but may be rather passive.

Margins: very narrow – lives life to the full,
generous.

Size: medium to large – generous, outgoing

Flow: very smooth – a quick thinker

Zones: slightly short upper zone. Because the writing is very legible and smoothly written, this is interpreted positively as self-reliant.

Slant: to the right, towards the future. Except in the lower zone, which has quite a strong pull backwards, to childhood, or a past experience.

Starting strokes: arcade style – yielding nature.

Ending strokes: none – likes to get on with the next job.

Connections: nearly all letters connected – quick mind.

Spacing: wide gaps between words – keeps people at a distance.

Direction: slightly rising – healthy, forward looking outlook, optimistic.

Pressure: medium – relaxed.

Speed: quite fast – quick witted.

'd': narrow loop – emotional repression.

'i': dot to right – impulsive.

'g': loops vary in style but all slant backwards – a pull away from acting on sensuality, perhaps a pull to some previous experience.

'I': varies a lot (an unusual feature) – very adaptable.

't': bar is short, to the right – likes to have some responsibility, but not to run the show.

Other observations: simplified letters (eg the capital 'T') show an uncluttered mind. A good organiser.

Capitals large: high self-regard.

Very open 'b's: a touch of naivety.

Summary:
This is a lively, active and adaptable person who enjoys life and is looking forward to the future. They are intelligent, self-reliant, and dislike elaboration and fuss. They would make an excellent organiser. On the emotional side they are reserved and inclined to let other people make the first move, and to keep people at a distance. There is some impulsiveness and naivety in their nature – at times they could be taken for a ride. This may be what happened in the past which would explain the emotional reserve indicated. They have good self-knowledge, and fairly high self-esteem.

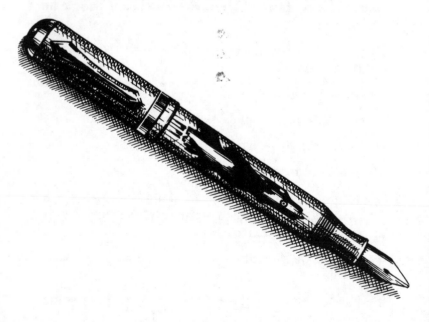

Taffeta phrases, silken three piled hyperboles, figures pedantical.

Study is like the sun, that will not be with fancy looks; sma plodders ever won, sma from others books. (Lo

Initial impressions: fairly legible, but many inconsistencies in letter size are readily apparent – enjoys variety and is quite adaptable.

Margins: reasonably even on left, full to the right: prepared to face the demands of the future.

Size: large – enjoys attention.

Flow: the writing is achieved rapidly and artfully, with a number of clever letter links and simplifications. This is an intelligent, fast thinker who has an inventive mind.

Zones: diminished upper zone. Like the previous example, the writing is legible and smoothly written, so this is interpreted positively as self-reliance.

Slant: upright, with a slight forward bias at times. Tends to respond to other people rather than initiate activity.

Starting strokes: none – likes to get on with the job, quite a practical, hands on person. Perhaps not a good planner.

Ending strokes: none – not good at farewells.

Connections: very high proportion of letters joined, in thread/garland style, and often in a quick, simplified stroke. Intelligent, fast thinking, imaginative.

Spacing: spaces between words are wide – does not let many people get close.

Direction: even line – emotionally stable.

Pressure: medium/heavy – energetic.

Speed: very fast – a sharp, incisive mind.

'd': open body – talkative. Spread stem – high view of own abilities.

'i': varies, but quite a few dash dots – enjoys change, can be very critical.

'g': open looped – desires unfulfilled.

'I': straight line – independent.

't': bar varies – showing an inconsistent control of willpower.

Other observations: open 'o's and 'a's show a talkative person. The crucifix shaped 'f' and occasional cruciform style 't', suggest a rather negative, fatalist attitude to life.

Some simplifications such as the 'v' shaped 'r's are overdone and suggest a wish to confuse people. This, combined with the secrecy loops in the 'd's, implies someone who creates an impression of mystique about themselves, who is talkative but not open.

Summary
This is a highly intelligent, creative person, a quick thinker with a critical mind. Although very active socially, they do not allow many people to get to know them well and deliberately hold back from saying too much about themselves. Emotionally they show a lack of fulfillment which may be a result of a passive, fatalist attitude. The emotional responses are not strong. Their high creativity and imagination and sense of being a 'free spirit' is perhaps being held back by a lack of drive.

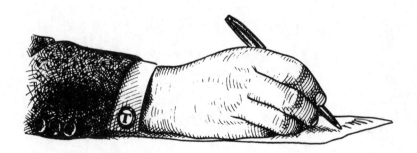

Theo van Doesburg. In

Dance' of 1918 we can

from the notion of a di

distinct areas using lin

which there is a free f

linear elements of the

which were originally es

paintings have been broke

inter link and overlap.

Initial impressions: very rigid, controlled writing, with many long, straight strokes – disciplined and controlled behaviour.

Margins: even with a slight narrowing on the left – a sign of drawing back from life at times.

Size: medium – conventional.

Flow: Despite the angular writing style, the script flows evenly across the page – balanced personality.

Zones: diminished lower zone. A sign of a lack of capacity to achieve what the writer wants to do. Probably a bit of a drifter.

Slant: upright – very controlled, the head ruling the heart, not very responsive.

Starting strokes: the vertical starting stroke on the 'p' is a sign of a stubborn nature.

Ending strokes: none – cool and abrupt.

Connections: these are very angular, showing an accurate and logical mind, and suggesting a degree of aggression. A high proportion of letters are printed, showing a reliance on intuition rather than planning.

Spacing: spaces between words are quite wide – does not let many people get close.

Direction: very straight line – keeps everything under strict control.

Pressure: heavy – aggressive.

Speed: medium to slow. Can be calculating.

'd': spread stem – strong belief in own abilities.

'i': placement very inconsistent – subject to mood changes.

'g': tick at bottom of a stright stem – lacking in

drive, tends to react to others. The tick indicates repressed aggression.

'I': straight and large – high self-image, imagination.

't': bar very low – not highly self-motivated.

Other observations: the 'o's and 'a's are closed which reveals a secretive nature. The Greek form 'e' suggests a love of culture, and the 'a's are also very artistic.

Summary
There is a sharp, alert mind in here, probably prone to sarcasm (all those angular ticks), with a very strong imagination. Although this person has strong self-belief, they lack drive and are dependent on other people to help them achieve what they want. They keep a strong control on their emotions and can be quite cold with people. They are also holding back a lot of aggression, which is bound to emerge in some form.

Various people have comm
find it very easy t
I found this problem be
I did a course in sh
any remnant of legibility

Initial impressions: rather scruffy, scrawly handwriting, suggesting a lack of attention to detail.

Margins: quite wide on the left, and narrow on the right. The writer is eager to get on.

Size: small script – intelligent, possible low self-image, can be inhibited.

Flow: rapidly written, not easy to read – suggests a degree of arrogance in the writer.

Zones: diminished middle zone. Avoids the limelight, but a very sharp and astute mind.

Slant: slightly leftwards – while not particularly introverted, the writer feels apart from and different to other people.

Starting strokes: none at all – keen to get started on things.

Ending strokes: some thread endings on words, a sign of shrewd intelligence.

Connections: thread style, many simplifications, some of them overdone, reducing legibility. Clever but not careful. Very high proportion of connected letters, indicating a fast, inventive mind.

Spacing: quite wide – people are kept at a distance.

Direction: slight rise in baseline – optimistic.

Pressure: medium – quite relaxed and easy going.

Speed: very fast – affects legibility. Can be impulsive.

'd': very narrow loop – inhibited.

'i': variable, with variable pressure. Sensitive and highly critical (lots of dashes).

'g': the 'g' loops vary but always have a slant to the right – a lively imagination and a reasonably developed sensuality which is kept very private. Not likely to throw a friendly arm around your shoulder!

'I': straight, left slant – independent, introspective.

't': bar only on right – dislikes restrictions.

Other observations: the 'o's are open, showing a talkative nature, but the secrecy loops, particularly on the 'd's suggest that this person does not talk about themselves very much. The 'p' open at the bottom reveals that the writer enjoys spending money.

Summary
The simplifications show intelligence but the lack of easy legibility reveals a certain arrogance – the writer does not care if people cannot quickly understand what they are saying, and moves on with the conversation. On the emotional side, this person does not like large groups and there is an element of inhibition in the writing. The writer has an astute mind and is a real 'doer', but there are some aspects

of their nature which are repressed. They are generous and socially competent, but do not let other people get too close to them. They may enjoy getting on with a job, but sometimes they do not cover every single aspect of it. Things can get left undone because they moved to the next task too early.

INDEX